africa dynamics

Specialists in travel to Africa

africa dynamics

Specialists in travel to Africa

We are proud to be associated with Wilderness Safaris and to share this wonderful publication with you.

Wildlife conservation in Africa is increasingly important for the generations to come. From the Cape to the Congo, Wilderness Safaris remains at the forefront of sustainable conservation in Africa.

Every visitor contributes strongly to the overall effort. We invite you to share this world with us …… if you have not been to Africa before it will be a journey beyond your imagining. And if you have, we know that you will be moved once again by the images and the majesty of Africa's great wilderness areas.

— www.africadynamics.com —

WILDERNESS volume 2

Wilderness, PO Box 5219, Rivonia, 2128, South Africa

www.wilderness.travel

Printed by: Tien Wah Press (PTE) Limited, Singapore

ISBN No: 978-0-620-52674-6

wildernesscontents

wildernessphilosophy

Skimmer Symbolism

The African Skimmer, called *Hahwerere* by the Bayei and *Kamungoma* by the Hambukushu people of the Okavango Delta, is also the symbol of Wilderness.

A distinctive bird, its striking black upperwings, pure white belly and bright yellow-orange bill are as diagnostic as its unique feeding behaviour. Individuals or flocks fly low in an effortless, buoyant style over Africa's water systems, dipping their bills into the water in a skimming motion designed to catch small fish close to the surface. Once a fish – usually less than 8cm in size – is detected, the bird's head and neck snap back in flight and the fish is secured in the bill. All of this takes place at speeds of up to 30 kilometres per hour!

Its efficient feeding belies the complexity of the species' evolutionary adaptation. The bill is a unique shape. The lower mandible – that part of the bill that skims the surface of the water – is nearly 40% longer than the upper. It is also incredibly thin and fused at the tip, with a rudder-like extension below this, so as to be aquadynamic and able to carve through the water without affecting flight.

Broad lowland rivers and lakes with exposed sandbanks for breeding are essential for their survival and the species moves widely in search of optimum conditions. African Skimmers are also sensitive to disturbance and habitat change. This leaves the species largely limited to protected areas in Africa where ecosystems continue to function as intended, and where rivers have not been impacted by damming or other hydrological schemes: in other words, wilderness.

For us, African Skimmers represent intact, pristine ecosystems in the most remote and productive parts of the continent. They are the essence of our name, soul and philosophy – that of Wilderness – and are incorporated into our logo in the form of their distinctive wing shape and flying style.

It is this wilderness that sustains us and which we believe is critical for humankind in the modern world. We want to ensure the survival of this wilderness and share it with others from across our planet. This is a belief we have held for 30 years, since the establishment of Wilderness Safaris in 1983.

About this book

Wilderness – Volume 2 is a tribute to the wilderness areas that we work in, and the biodiversity and people that they support. We hope this catalogue of landscapes, stories, places, journeys and species will inspire you as it does us.

wildernessmoments

wilderness moments

wildernessmoments

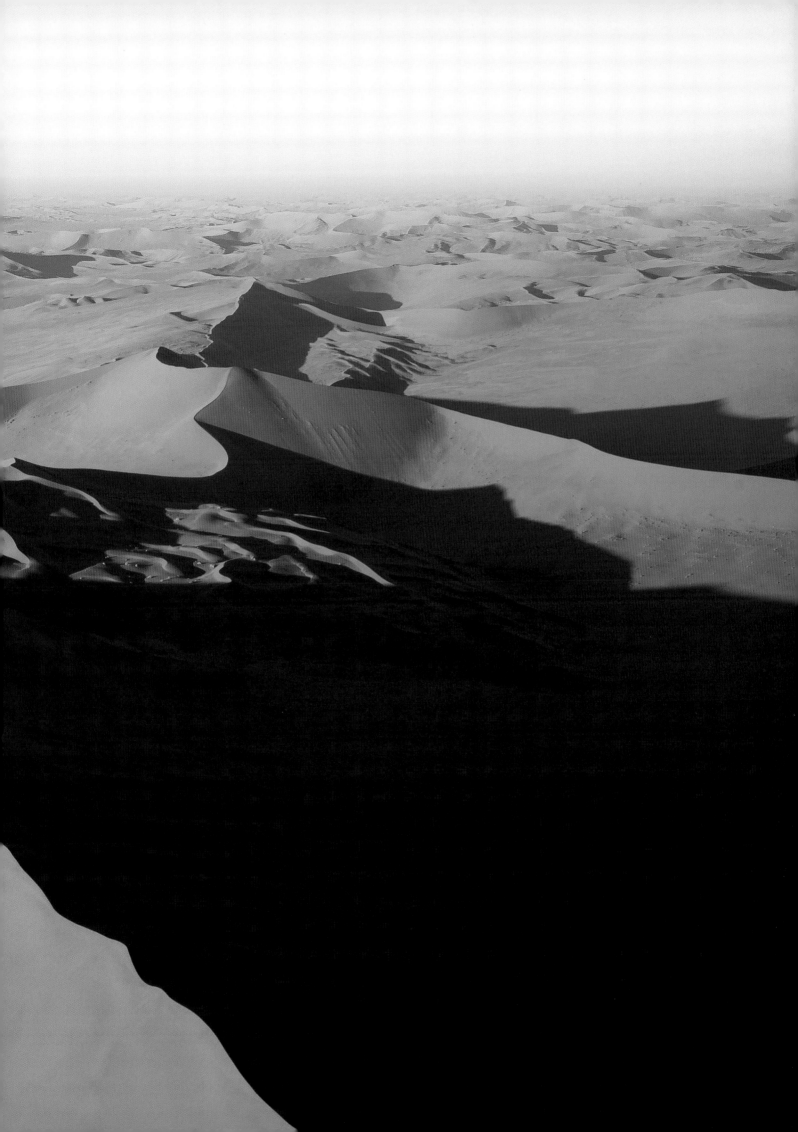

wilderness moments

wildernessmoments

wildernessmoments

wildernessmoments

wilderness moments

wilderness**moments**

wildernesscongo

Rainforest Treasure Chest
Odzala-Kokoua National Park

Rainforests are a vitally significant part of life on Earth. Not only do they play a pivotal role in the absorption of carbon dioxide and thus in regulating global climate, but they are also treasure chests of biodiversity vital for the resilience of our planet. The Congo Basin, the world's second largest expanse of tropical rainforest, extends across six central African countries and provides shelter for no fewer than 10 000 plant, 1 000 bird, 700 fish and 400 mammal species. Like the Amazon and other tropical rainforests, however, it is under immense pressure from logging, mining, the bushmeat trade and further threats. By opening two camps in Odzala-Kokoua National Park in Congo (Brazzaville), we hope to help arrest these impacts by raising the profile of the region and establishing alternative livelihoods through ecotourism.

Megafauna of the Forest

Rainforests are famous for their staggering diversity, with unimaginable numbers of plant, bird and insect species per hectare. While large charismatic mammals are rare in rainforests and seem rather to belong to the savannah, Africa is different: forest elephants, for example – a distinct and slightly smaller species than their savannah cousins – are the 'gardeners' of the forest, with many trees depending on elephant digestive systems for seed dispersal and germination. Other megafauna include the forest buffalo – an exotic red variation of the savannah form – which are as imposing when viewed close up on foot; the bongo, whose impressive bulk rivals that of its relative the eland; and, of course, the most compelling forest creature of all: the 180kg (390lb) silverback gorilla.

wildernesscongo

Parrots and Pigeons
Many-feathered multitude of Lango Bai

Aside from large mammals, Lango Bai attracts two colourful, charismatic bird species: African Grey Parrots and African Green-Pigeons. These spectacular avian visitors arrive every morning in their thousands, providing an incredible visual and aural display.

As the sun rises, small flocks of parrots gather in a stand of tall trees next to the bai. Their loud whistling and screeching betrays their nervousness and for more than an hour they goad each other, until eventually the braver birds scout the open patch of clay and mud at the edge of the bai and alight. Once on the ground, the adventurous individuals become a noisy, almost chaotic frenzy as the parrots feed on the open soil. The contrast between their bright red tails, white rumps and smooth grey upper parts is as striking as that between their sociability in the wild and the loneliness of the captive cage bird.

At the same time, further down the bai system, the almost deafening cascading sound of countless wings signals the arrival of a thousand Green-Pigeons, the slightest alarm causing a panicked circling of the area by the swollen flock before they settle again. They too are nervous of predators, such as the Black Sparrowhawk and other fast-flying raptors.

Both species are largely frugivorous in their diet. Unripe fruit and the toxins in seeds were once thought to be problematic to their digestion, and clay proposed as crucial to their wellbeing since it may help absorb or purge these chemicals. The latest research, however, suggests that the birds are actually in search of clay with high sodium content, since this mineral salt is lacking in their diet and is a nutrient essential to their survival.

Gorillas in our Midst

Western lowland gorillas of the Congo

After chimpanzees and bonobos, gorillas are our closest relatives, with some genetic studies suggesting that we share more than 97% of our DNA with the largest of the world's great apes. Whatever the genetic overlap, there is a mutual fascination between the species: in 1970, intimate images of Dian Fossey interacting with curious Rwanda mountain gorillas featured on the cover of *National Geographic* magazine and captured the imagination of the world.

There are two gorilla species in Africa, each comprising two subspecies. The eastern gorilla, *Gorilla beringei* (categorised as Endangered by the IUCN), includes the well-known mountain gorillas of Rwanda and Uganda, as well as the eastern lowland gorilla of the Democratic Republic of Congo. The western gorilla, *Gorilla gorilla* (Critically Endangered), includes the western lowland gorilla, found primarily in Congo (Brazzaville) and Gabon, and the Cross River gorilla of Cameroon and Nigeria.

Odzala has the highest reported densities of the western lowland gorilla. In the mid-1990s this factor and the very low human population attracted Dr Magda Bermejo and her partner German Illera to the region to begin an in-depth field study of this almost mythical animal. Magda was the first to successfully habituate western lowland gorillas to humans, a breakthrough that enabled major advances in studies of their range and ecology. She has continued her pioneering work for nearly twenty years, and is currently studying a new gorilla community in the Ndzehi area adjacent to Odzala.

Here Magda and German have encountered extremely high gorilla densities and have been able to habituate a number of groups to the presence of researchers and small groups of ecotourists staying at Ngaga Camp in the middle of this pristine forest. Extraordinarily skilled Mbeti trackers methodically follow the trails of gorilla groups on a daily basis, allowing us an intimate, almost voyeuristic, glimpse into the lives of these dignified, gentle apes with whom we share so much.

Winged Wonders

Butterflies of Odzala

Butterflies are abundant in tropical rainforests, with hundreds of species of varying sizes occupying subtly different niches at every height. Odzala is no different: the southern parts are home to more than 700 species in excess of 150 genera, ranging from the continent's largest, the African giant swallowtail, with a wingspan of more than 20 centimetres, to the diminutive members of the Lycaenidae. Many of Odzala's species gather in spectacular clouds in forest clearings and edges, where sunlight, moisture and minerals combine to attract these striking insects as they seek out salts critical to their diet.

wildernesscongo

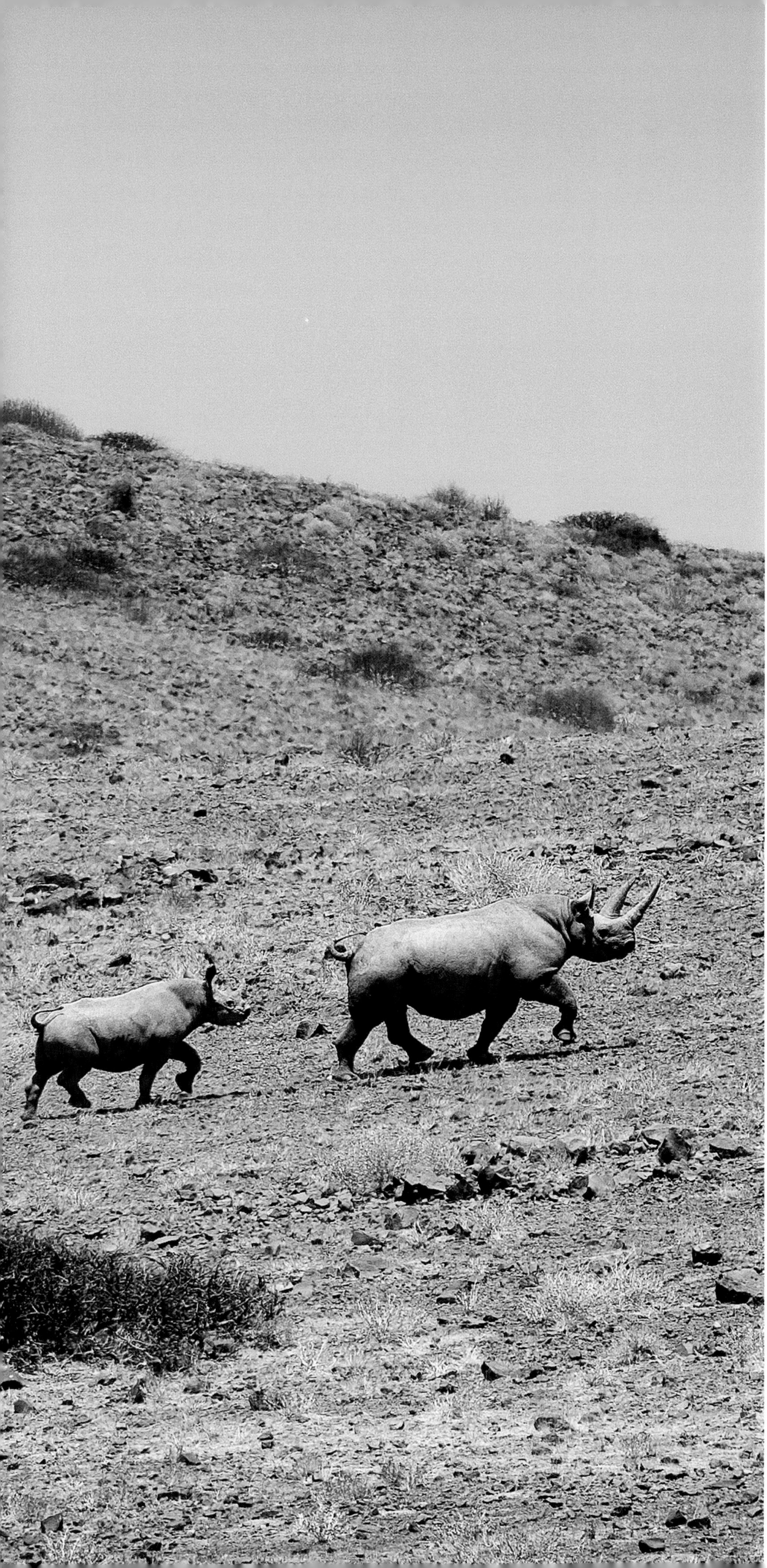

wildernessnamibia

Wealth of Cultures
Namibia's people

Namibia's two million-strong population comprises nine major ethnic groups, with the Ovambo making up half the population. Herero and Himba people are perhaps the most visually distinctive, the women of the former group unmistakable in heavy Victorian-style dresses, petticoats and characteristic wide and colourful hats. The Himba on the other hand seem to live on the edge of time, their unusual dress with fine leatherwork and intricate hairstyles identifying them as traditionalists clinging steadfastly to a long-established way of life. In Damaraland, Nama, Damara and Riemvasmaker live side by side, each proud of their unique heritage.

wildernessnamibia

Sun-Lovers of the Sands
Lizards of Namibia

The driest regions of Namibia are ironically richest in endemism and host some of the most interesting elements of the country's biodiversity. As is fitting for such a dry, hot place, there are more species of reptiles than mammals, and more sun-loving lizards (125 species) than anywhere else on the continent.

Every niche seems to be filled by an endemic or near-endemic reptile, in the rocky plains and hillsides, sand dunes, riverbeds and shrub vegetation. The adaptations of these creatures are numerous and wondrous: from Anchieta's dune lizard with its peculiar thermoregulatory dance to the colour-changing Namaqua chameleon. The striking translucence of the web-footed gecko contrasts with the cryptically coloured ground agama, and even more so, the colourful Namibian rock agama. The camouflaged and attractive Boulton's Namib day gecko is relatively easy to find when compared with the various barking geckos whose mysterious and ventriloquial calls punctuate the dusk.

Carnivore Tug of War
Etosha waterhole drama

The waterholes of Ongava and neighbouring Etosha are hubs of activity in the dry season, throngs of springbok, gemsbok, blue wildebeest, plains zebra, giraffe, greater kudu and other species drawn inexorably to their life-giving waters. As a result, they are also the inevitable scenes of dramatic species interactions, as these images taken at Gemsbokvlakte Waterhole in Etosha National Park in September show.

A pair of opportunistic black-backed jackals seized hold of a springbok that had come to drink and, in the struggle to bring it down, attracted more jackals. Finally, the springbok weakened and drowned and a total of nine jackals attempted to drag it out of the water.

Before they could reap the benefits, however, their squabbles attracted the attention of two magnificent male lions, who charged onto the scene and drove the smaller carnivores off. Their superior size meant that they could lift the carcass easily out of the water, but the ensuing tussle over it left one with the 'lion's share,' while the other had to be content with the tail end!

What was additionally interesting – aside from the dramatic demonstration of the carnivore hierarchy – was the nonchalant way in which life continued for the rest of the herbivore spectators (springbok and gemsbok) as they waited their turn to drink.

Nest of a Near-Endemic
White-tailed Shrike

The bizarre White-tailed Shrike, *Lanioturdus torquatus*, an enigmatic near-endemic to northern and central Namibia (with a minor extension into south-western Angola), is a real 'tick' for birders. Apart from its restricted distribution, it is also taxonomically intriguing, demonstrating some affinities to the bush-shrikes, sharing many characteristics with the batises, and designated – confusingly – through its genus as a shrike-thrush – *Lanioturdus*.

Although egg-laying can occur year round, nesting apparently peaks about November; this nest, in a purple-pod terminalia, mostly devoid of leaves prior to the onset of the rainy season, was found on the Ongava Reserve at that time.

The nest, a shallow cup of neatly woven twigs, grass and spider web, was placed in the fork of the tree about 2.5 metres off the ground. Its colouration perfectly matched that of the tree bark and no additional camouflage appeared to be used.

Over a two-day period, guide and guests watched from a respectful distance as the parents fed the two chicks. Intervals between feeding were generally around 30 minutes, the parents' arrival betrayed by distinctive calling (best described as loud whistles) as they clumsily flew in with large white wing-flashes. They would then rapidly deliver the food: mostly butterflies, small caterpillars, termites and even the odd spider. As soon as the chicks sensed that the parents were nearby, they would instantly open their beaks towards the sky and make noisy begging calls.

The parents were also observed removing the faecal sacs of the nestlings, thus improving nest sanitation and reducing the chance of detection by would-be predators – characteristic behaviour of passerines whose young remain on the nest for longer periods. In the early morning, one of the adults was seen sitting on the nest, possibly helping to regulate the temperature of the chicks as they were still essentially blind, naked and helpless.

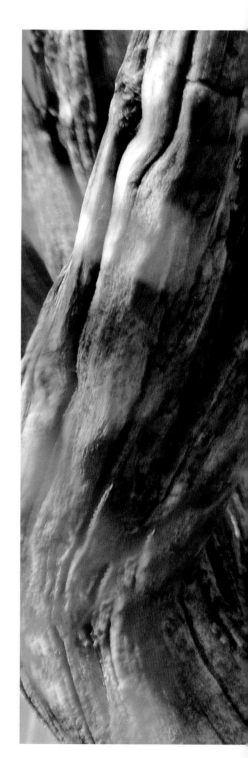

Partnering for Conservation

Doro !Nawas Community Conservancy

Although Namibia enjoys one of the lowest population densities in the world, there is no doubt that the people here play as important a role in the successes of conservation as anywhere else in Africa. In fact, given that in so many cases land is shared between wildlife and people, rural communities are overwhelmingly the central tenet of Namibian conservation.

Nowhere is this truer than in the community conservancies. Here, in a seminal innovation by both government and communities, large areas of small-scale pastoral farming have been brought under wildlife, with successful ecotourism the most important revenue earner and employer for the communities. Wilderness has been an important part of this process since the mid-1990s and is the private-sector ecotourism partner in a joint-venture partnership (Doro Nawas Camp) in the Doro !Nawas Conservancy, Kunene Region.

Registered in December 1999, Doro !Nawas is a well-established, 407 300-hectare community conservancy adjacent to the well-known rock engraving site of Twyfelfontein and home to

the Petrified Forest, desert-adapted elephant and other wildlife, as well as some 1 500 community members.

In 2009, Wilderness and the Doro !Nawas Conservancy signed a shareholding agreement allowing a landlord/tenant relationship to evolve into one where the conservancy not only receives a percentage of revenue from Doro Nawas Camp but is also a shareholder in the business.

In addition to community-centric employment and training, and the revenue share that resulted from the former partnership, the Doro !Nawas Conservancy now also receives dividends from its shareholding in the ecotourism business and is an active executive member of the partnership. Revenue from Doro Nawas Camp and other conservancy initiatives has allowed reinvestment in employment and important community projects in the area, and has proved the dictum that responsible ecotourism conducted in partnership with rural communities can be both a local economic engine as well as a conservation mechanism.

Rain in the Desert

Rainfall in Namibia is scarce, measuring less than 50mm a year at the coast, and paltry 50-100mm inland annually. But when it does rain, the shade, tint and even the shape of the land change dramatically: verdant green grasses soften the horizon, leaves glisten in the sunlight, and small bushes burst with bright yellow flowers. Change is almost immediate, whole landscapes transforming literally overnight. The most extraordinary transformation is perhaps at Sossusvlei. Ironically, the Nama-derived name means "the gathering place of water" – in good years seasonal rains in the foothills of the Naukluft and Tsaris Mountains can reach the vlei, where the water persists for a while, mirroring perfectly the skies and green-red dunes around them.

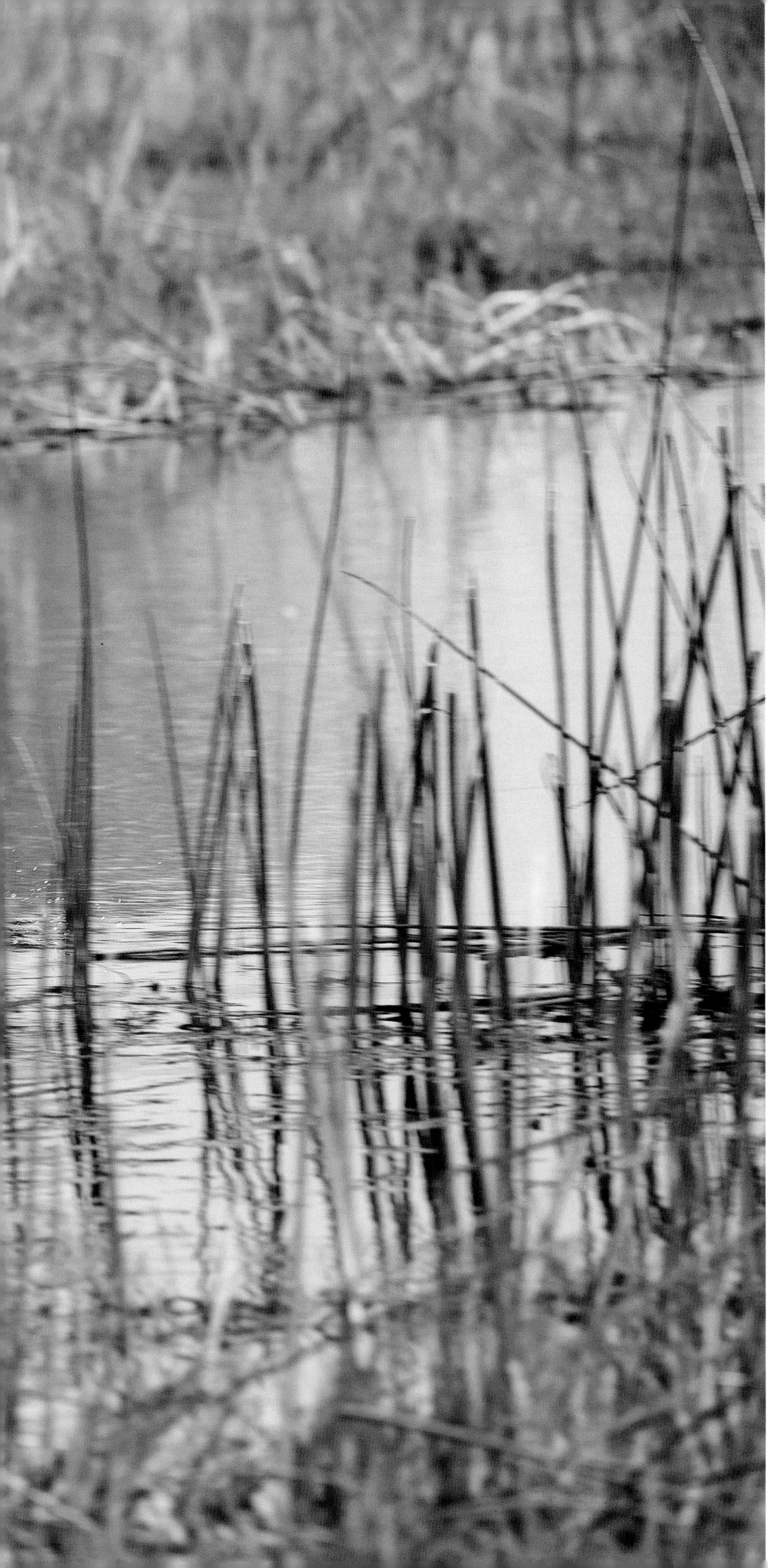

wildernessbotswana

Delta Diversity

The Okavango is the largest inland delta system in the world, an area of 15 000 square kilometres patterned by channels, lagoons, swamps and islands. Reeds and papyrus beds capture sediment as they filter the water, creating crystal clarity and a sweetness of taste that heightens the sense that this is somehow a miracle – an otherwise arid place that receives its water in Botswana's dry season. Only after summer rainfall has ceased do the floodwaters arrive in the Delta from further north, creating a fertile oasis crammed with life. This phenomenon forms one of the most incredible wildlife sanctuaries in Africa, with a huge diversity of fauna and flora: delicate reed frogs, secretive sitatunga, lily-trotting jacanas and a plethora of other life.

Mombo's Lone Wild Dog
An anomaly in interspecies relationships

In the mid-1990s the dominant predator in the Mombo area was the wild dog; at the peak, one pack numbered more than 40 animals. The wild dog reign was ended by a surge in the spotted hyaena population, followed by an increase in lion, today's principal predator. For the past decade lion and hyaena have held sway and wild dogs have been only transitory visitors, moving on to avoid confrontation.

Bizarrely, a single female wild dog has proven the exception to the rule. Since her arrival in early 2009 she has defied the odds. Not only does she manage to survive in an area with very high densities of far larger, more powerful predators, but she does so on her own. She is a very successful hunter – a notable feat considering that wild dogs are highly sociable animals that hunt in packs – and has settled down to a stable home range just east of Mombo Camp. The gregarious nature of the species quickly became apparent as this lone female sought out other canid company and established an unusual relationship with first one, then a number of black-backed jackal pairs in the area. At first she was merely tolerated and followed by both jackal and spotted hyaena for scavenging purposes, but when one of the jackal pairs produced pups, the wild dog began to regurgitate food for the hungry puppies as she would have done for her own. She even urged the adult jackals to accompany her on hunts.

The original jackal pups have reached adulthood, but they still recognise the wild dog as a source of food. Indeed she actively encourages them: several jackals have been seen 'greeting' her in precisely the way that wild dog packs do before setting off on a hunt. Faster than the jackals, she kills alone, and then either vocalises or runs back to guide them to the carcass. On one occasion she carried meat across water too deep for the waiting jackals on the other side! Up to nine jackals have been seen attending one of her kills.

She now associates with three different pairs of jackals and their offspring, never resting or sleeping without at least one jackal close by, which suggests that perhaps one of the reasons for the relationship is security – the wild dog provides food in return for the anti-predatory benefits of sociality: more eyes and ears to watch for lion. Her relationship with hyaena is harder to fathom – there are at least two individuals she tolerates (she greets them nose to nose), and has been seen to share a kill with the clan's dominant female. It is quite a sight to witness three different species forming a hunting party as they set off: one dog accompanied by bouncing jackals, and a hyaena or two loping behind.

The Greening of Xigera

Solar energy at Wilderness

Since 2009, and in constantly striving for a lighter ecological footprint, all new Wilderness camps have been powered fully by solar energy. At the same time we are pursuing a programme of retrofitting existing camps with renewable energy systems: hot water and electricity entirely supplied by solar power through inverter and battery systems, with generators for back-up only.

Xigera, in the heart of the Okavango Delta, is also part of the heart of Wilderness, and since its inception in 1985 has been dependent on diesel generators for its power requirements. On 13 June 2011, the generators were turned off and the power for the entire camp was switched across to a new photovoltaic solar plant, consisting of a total of 135 solar panels, which produce a maximum of 30 kilowatts of renewable energy – enough power from the sun to run the entire camp, including all fridges and freezers.

To heat water, existing geysers in the camp already used the sun, but were hampered by the heavy shade of the island's trees. To counter this, state-of-the-art thermodynamic geysers were installed: extremely efficient heat-pumps (with a tiny compressor requiring very little power) that extract warmth from the air and use it to heat the water. These geysers are so efficient that they can produce hot water at any time of day or night throughout the year, and they require less than one fifth of the power of a conventional electric geyser!

In Botswana, Xigera joins Zarafa, Selinda, Kalahari Plains, Banoka Bush Camp and Mombo in being fully solar-powered, while plans for further installations at Vumbura Plains, DumaTau, Kings Pool and other camps are in progress.

wildernessbotswana

Miniature Militia
Mongooses of Botswana

Small yet fierce, the mongoose family has long been a symbol of valour and courage, often against foes (and prey) twice their size. Perhaps it is their renowned combative engagement of venomous snakes for which they are most celebrated, but the eight different mongoose species occurring in northern Botswana occupy a variety of niches and prey on vastly different creatures. The most abundant terrestrial species typically prey on a range of beetles, scorpions, skinks, rodents, ground-nesting birds and snakes, while the water mongoose is a crab specialist, and some species may even take prey as large as a scrub hare.

Piscatorial Paradise
Waterbirds of the Okavango Delta

The waters of the Okavango Delta, as a result of their annual ebb and flow, are a magnet for fish-eating birds. Each year, as the seasonal inundation arrives and advances over the floodplains, different fish species take the opportunity to spawn, the ephemeral nature of the 'new' habitat providing a refuge against traditional predators. In this transitional period the fingerlings are able to grow to a size that enables them to migrate back to prime habitat as the floodplains dry out towards the end of the dry season. It is then that so-called "fish traps" form. As the waters recede, fish of all sizes are caught in the remaining pools and are preyed upon by dramatic concentrations of herons, storks, pelicans, egrets, fish eagles and other piscivorous birds. Prior to this glut, however, different species stake out their respective watery niches and use a combination of patience, stealth and surprise to take their toll on the next generation of the Delta's fish population.

Unique to the Okavango Delta, the catfish run happens each year, starting in early August and ending in November. During this period, the receding water levels concentrate the smaller fish species, causing predatory catfish to gather in their hundreds and work their way upstream as they hunt. In their wake, they attract an eager supporting cast of waterbirds that also congregate in equally impressive numbers to feed on any remaining survivors.

An Elephant Birth
Warona joins the Abu Herd

At just after 10pm on Saturday, 17 December 2011, Shireni, one of the adult elephant cows at Abu Camp, gave birth to a female calf. Staff and guests braved the bad weather to witness the tiny animal's first moments. Finding her feet in the pouring rain was a slippery challenge for the newborn, but, to everyone's delight, after 20 minutes she stood, wobbling slightly. The other six elephants of the Abu herd rumbled through the night, no doubt spreading the news to the wilderness beyond.

The elephant handlers named her Warona, a Setswana word meaning "for us." Reaching up to her mother, Warona suckled properly for the first time at 7am the next morning, 10 hours after the birth.

The first day was filled with excitement. Her first attempt at leaving the boma was short-lived; after just six steps she flopped over and had a twenty-minute nap – clearly getting moving is a big effort for an elephant just a few hours old. After a while Shireni gently woke her up and, with the help of Cathy, the matriarch of the herd, got her to her feet and on the move again. This time they got out the gates, across the dry riverbed and out into the green bush to the north of camp.

All watched as her bandy rubber legs quivered and gave in again and again; each time one of the other elephants was there to help her back on her feet, the herd always surrounding and protecting her, stroking her with their trunks, never letting her out of their sight.

The elephants meandered slowly through the bush, constantly checking on their newest member. By lunchtime, Paseka, the troublesome two-year-old, and Warona were napping under a tree, while Cathy, Shireni and Abu stood over them, keeping watch.

Sharing Knowledge
Training in the Wilderness

Wilderness is known for its striking wilderness areas – but no less for the warmth and hospitality of its staff, from camp manager to camp hand. Wilderness staff are committed to making a difference to people's lives and the world around them. Our camps and safaris are hosted by individuals who love what they do. Our guides are the link between our guests and the intricacies of the natural world, and they share their knowledge with passion and humour.

Staff training is therefore a vital part of our operation: through a comprehensive training programme, we aim to provide our people with the skills to become some of the best guides and managers in Africa. In Botswana, the Wilderness Training Division has its own camp (Kaparota) in the Okavango, used exclusively for training courses. Entry-level camp manager or guiding courses last a month, with students then going on to complete eight-month internships in the camps, where they are periodically assessed by the training team while on the job until each module in either guiding or camp management has been passed. In the guiding field, after passing Level 1 of the Wilderness Training Standard, guides can advance further by participating in intensive ten-day courses in specialised skills.

In this way dedicated guides, naturalists and managers share their knowledge with the next generation of staff. The results speak for themselves, as Botswana guides have rapidly gained the reputation of being amongst the finest in Africa.

98

The Fast and the Furry

While the quintessential Kalahari image for many is of a large black-maned male lion striding across the plains, there are a host of smaller carnivores that have adapted to the vagaries of this sometimes harsh land. The cheetah is perhaps the best known, a sleek and fast spotted carnivore, well adapted to the open terrain. Less well-known species include the predominantly nocturnal brown hyaena, intimidating honey badger, and the large-eared Cape fox and bat-eared fox. Daylight sightings of these usually secretive species are more common than one would think, with badgers and bat-eared foxes regular visitors to the plain in front of Kalahari Plains Camp.

100

wildernesszimbabwe

David versus Goliath
Conflict in a shrinking Mana pool

The four large pools of Mana Pools National Park after which the Park is named (*mana* means 'four' in Shona) are remnant channels of the Zambezi River now separated from the main flow. They hold water all year round and attract all manner of wildlife and waterfowl during the dry season. However, before the annual summer rains, both water and food resources become scarce and competition between species intensifies.

Marabou Storks, the largest member of this family, typically feed on carrion, but with their imposing size and specialised bill structure, they are also highly opportunistic – taking varied food items such as fish, birds, amphibians and snakes. They are also very efficient at stealing prey from other birds in aggressive interactions.

As pictured at right, avian "David and Goliath" duels between smaller Yellow-billed Storks and the larger Marabous are regular, the smaller bird using its agility in flight to escape its larger opponent, prey intact.

Carnivore Competition
Mana's large predator guild

The fertile floodplain of Mana Pools National Park hosts large concentrations of wildlife, particularly in the dry season, when the waters of the Zambezi River are a magnet for mammals. Buffalo, zebra, impala, warthog, eland, waterbuck, greater kudu, bushbuck and even leviathan hippo all fall prey to a full range of large predators. Lion, spotted hyaena, leopard, wild dog and cheetah each carve out specific niches in this crowded ecosystem – in terms of habitat, daily activity peaks and prey selection – in order to avoid competition and conflict.

wildernesszimbabwe

Parched Plain

Ngamo, Hwange National Park

An area of only 12 square kilometres, Ngamo Plains in the south-east corner of Hwange is disproportionately productive. Rich thickets of acacia woodland fringe an open plain: luxuriantly grassy in summer, parched and arid in winter.

It is perhaps in the dry season that the plain is at its most evocative. Long lines of zebra or wildebeest trudge their way through the dust to the permanent waterhole, herds of eland and impala delicately pluck acacia pods, and sentinel giraffe survey what appears to be a desolate landscape.

Even Hwange's elephant herds seek out Ngamo's water, breeding herds appearing from the surrounding woodlands like ghostly apparitions shrouded in the fine grey dust of the plain.

Spotted and Secretive
Cheetah in Hwange

The cheetah is a superbly specialised carnivore, uniquely adapted for relatively long, high-speed chases of small- and medium-sized antelope. As a result they have an enviable success rate in their hunts. They are also relatively slight and timid in comparison to the more powerful species of lion and spotted hyaena with whom they must share their ranges.

In order to lessen the risk of losing hard-won kills and occasionally even the lives of cubs, subadults and unwary adults, cheetah are predominantly diurnal. They also avoid areas of high lion density and are generally secretive and unobtrusive across very large home ranges.

They are thus not often seen and sightings are unpredictable, especially in the prime lion areas of south-east Hwange National Park. Here, cheetah relish the open, game-rich plains, but are able to use these areas only in the absence of lion. Instead they are seen more often in the vast woodland areas with lower prey numbers and thus fewer lion. Here, there is a higher chance of cub survival and they eke out an existence away from competing carnivores.

Teach Teachers, Build Schools
Hwange schools rehabilitation

Zimbabwe's economic woes of the last few years have had an effect on every aspect of society and education in remote areas has been particularly hard hit. Slashed budgets, emigrating teachers and crumbling facilities have all had an impact on the level of education for rural children.

Noting the seriousness of the impact, Children in the Wilderness (CITW) Zimbabwe decided to extend its regular environmental education programme to begin helping children in their communities and in their schools. The first intervention saw the launch of a feeding programme (where more than 1 200 children are given a meal every day of the school year), which was followed by a school rehabilitation programme at four schools – Ziga, Mpindo, Kapane and Ngamo – all of which are situated on the south-eastern border of the Hwange National Park.

Mindful of the shortage of teaching skills, the project first pulled in the help of O- and A-level school leavers to teach under instruction from the headmasters, and paid their wages. With salaries supplemented by CITW, better qualified teachers began to return and

teacher training programmes were then implemented with comprehensive curricula, lesson notes and practical exercises provided. An annual three-week literacy and environmental teacher training workshop sees a number of American teachers and volunteers arrive to give of their time and expertise.

A full survey of the community school facilities established the enormity of the rehabilitation needs. As a result, new classrooms have been built and books, stationery and even desks and chairs brought in for each school. Indeed, for the first time in its history, Ziga School won awards from the Ministry of Education for the best Grade 7 results in a small rural school in Matabeleland and for being the most enterprising school in the district!

Of course, facilities and teachers are one thing; without water, education becomes secondary. Accordingly, the first boreholes have been sunk in order to provide fresh water for the purposes of health, diet and cleanliness. Not only does fresh water keep children and teachers hydrated, but it also provides water for the new vegetable garden that supplies the feeding project.

.

Great Grey Giants
Hwange's 30 000 elephants

More than 30 000 giant grey pachyderms roam the 15 000 square kilometre Hwange National Park. These elephants are iconic and synonymous with Hwange, the extent of their dry season concentrations renowned across Africa.

During the dry southern hemisphere winter, pans, waterholes and other seasonal water sources across the National Park begin to shrink and ultimately to dry up. The dwindling water sources then attract higher and higher concentrations of animals, not only of elephant, but also of all other water-dependent herbivore species: buffalo, sable, zebra, impala, waterbuck and giraffe being among the most visible.

It is the elephants that dominate the landscape, however. Large herds, calves running excitedly ahead of their mothers, converge on water sources in the late afternoon and early evening, the different colours of the dust on their backs betraying the varied origins of their long journeys.

wildernesszambia

Seasonal Reprieve

Summer's arrival in Busanga

After a long, sometimes hot, always dusty, dry season, Africa's thirsty landscapes yearn for rain. Such longing builds in tandem with the blooming of swollen cumulus clouds on the horizon and eventually, after weeks of pregnant anticipation, the inertia is broken with the first showers and downpours of the summer months, the smell of moist soil often sensed before the first raindrops arrive.

On the Busanga Plains, in remote north-western Kafue National Park, the arrival of summer is dramatic. Towering dark clouds gather and brood above the vast dry floodplain, lightning dissecting the sky, until the advancing tempest drenches the ground, bringing life back to its parched crust.

It is only then that the land becomes inundated, a new seasonal cycle dominated by waterlilies, aquatic birds, amphibians and myriad fish, lasting throughout the summer until evaporation and drainage transform the colours of the Plains once more.

wildernesszambia

Hooves and Horns
Antelope of Kafue National Park

Visitors to the Busanga Plains leave with memories of large red lechwe and puku herds silhouetted in the early morning mists and orange haze of the spectacular Kafue dawns. This is, however, just a small taste of the varied antelope diversity that can be encountered here.

In the north-west lie the Busanga Swamps, a papyrus-dominated wetland that has a healthy sitatunga population and is one of the easier places in Africa for patient observers to view this specialist antelope. The most aquatic of all antelope and related to bushbuck and kudu, any sighting of sitatunga is prized due to their secretive and often nocturnal habits.

The swamps give way to the vast seasonally-inundated grassland of the Busanga Plains, the favoured haunt of similarly water-loving lechwe, southern reedbuck and puku, which are joined in the dry season by good numbers of roan antelope. Blue wildebeest are also frequently observed along the treeline bordering the plains, together with species such as greater kudu and impala. This treeline fringe and further south in the Park, where *Brachystegia* woodland and grassy dambos can be found, are ideal for more reclusive species such as Lichtenstein's hartebeest, defassa waterbuck and oribi. At the driest time of year even the majestic sable antelope leaves the surrounding woodlands to seek water on the plains, adding to the area's diversity.

Kings without Kingdoms
The Kafue Lion Project

Despite their legendary cultural ubiquity, lion are in danger, with estimates of between 20 000 and 30 000 individuals remaining across the entire African continent. They have been extirpated from over 80% of their former range. At 22 500 square kilometres, Kafue National Park is a potential stronghold, yet very little is known about the status of lion in the Park and in the surrounding Game Management Areas. This situation led to the 2010 establishment of the Kafue Lion Project, an initiative to investigate the conservation status of Kafue's lion population, as well as to identify potential threats to the species in the greater Kafue ecosystem.

Unfortunately, lion are notoriously difficult to count. In order to arrive at an estimate of lion density for Kafue, a combination of survey techniques is being used, including call-up surveys (where buffalo distress calls are played at specific points and responding predators are recorded), spoor count surveys, prey abundance counts, and GPS collars being fitted across three prides of females and three territorial male coalitions. With poaching, fire, flooding, disease and hunting forming a suite of potential threats, the spatial data provided will assist in determining which, if any, of these factors is limiting lion numbers in the Park and its surrounds.

The Project is an example of collaboration between ecotourism, NGOs, academia and government: Wilderness Safaris, Wilderness Wildlife Trust, Panthera (an NGO dedicated to wild cat conservation), South Africa's University of Cape Town and the Zambia Wildlife Authority (ZAWA) are all involved in and contributing to this study.

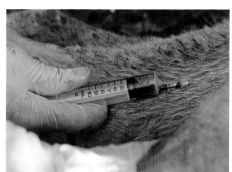
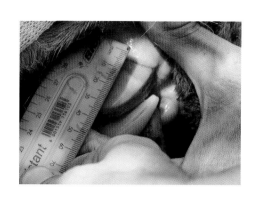

Magical Miombo
Threatened woodland

"Miombo" is a term used to describe a specialised, deciduous, moist broad-leafed woodland community dominated by trees belonging to the *Brachystegia*, *Julbernardia* and *Isoberlinia* families. This woodland type is essentially restricted to Angola, southern Tanzania, Zimbabwe, Malawi and Mozambique, with vast areas covering Zambia. Within miombo, towering trees are bedecked in old man's beard lichens and epiphytic orchids. A rich leaf litter adds an equally intriguing understorey of pretty grasses and flowers. It is perhaps most captivating at the end of the dry season when the trees' new leaves blush in gold and red hues before turning green.

Many bird species are restricted to miombo, and this unique woodland offers some of Africa's most rewarding birding opportunities, particularly when encountering mixed-species feeding flocks of up to 25 species! These can include Miombo Rock-Thrush, Rufous-bellied Tit, Red-capped Crombec, Böhm's Flycatcher, Yellow-bellied Hyliota, Spotted Creeper, Souza's Shrike and Western Violet-backed Sunbird, to mention a few. Mammals such as Lichtenstein's hartebeest, sable antelope and African wild dog also favour this habitat.

Miombo woodland is unfortunately under extreme threat. Rural communities depend on the wood they cut as a primary fuel source, while there is a dramatically growing demand for charcoal from these woods in burgeoning urban areas. As the soils are relatively nutrient-poor, slash-and-burn subsistence agriculture exacts a heavy toll when new lands for crops are opened each season. Zambia's Kafue National Park, cloaked in pristine tracts of this threatened woodland, is thus critical for its future conservation.

136

Clash of the Titans

The hippo density in the Luangwa River in South Luangwa National Park is one of Africa's highest, with more than 50 animals per kilometre along some stretches. As the dry season progresses and the river narrows, leaving reduced suitable daytime habitat in its deeper pools and bends, different pods are forced to crowd together and tempers can fray, bulls imposing dominance on interlopers and rival males through their two-ton bulk and formidable canines and incisors.

Living and Learning in Luangwa
Ecotourism and employment in Malama Chiefdom

Zambia's Eastern Province, in which the South Luangwa National Park is situated, is remote and poor, with very few employment prospects. Here, human-animal conflict is common, making agriculture difficult and sometimes risky; tsetse flies inhibit livestock farming and harsh conditions make even subsistence agriculture a challenge. One of the few employment opportunities available is in ecotourism and, with 70% of Kalamu Lagoon Camp's 23 staff members coming from villages in the Malama Chiefdom on the eastern boundary of the Park, Wilderness plays an important role in the community.

A staff survey conducted by Wilderness Community and Culture Coordinator Sue Snyman in October 2010 revealed that employment at Kalamu Lagoon Camp is critical in terms of income earned, its role in poverty reduction and improving overall social welfare. It

also enables people to work near their homes. This is especially relevant in terms of recent trends towards urbanisation and plays an important part in keeping families together, creating more stable family structures.

Aside from the direct impact of salaries and the multiplier effects of camp and staff spending, the calculated average of 7.27 dependents per staff member means that a high number of people (approximately 167) are indirectly supported by this one camp. But there is more to the positive effect of Kalamu Lagoon than these numbers. The improved social welfare of our staff is substantial and includes HIV testing (100% of Wilderness staff respondents know their HIV status), balanced meals while on duty, and the ability to build better houses and afford tertiary education for their children and other family members.

Meanwhile, guests of Kalamu, who are offered guided visits to the community, have been inspired to help invest in village infrastructure, particularly with regard to children and education. In this way, a community library at Kalengo Primary School has been built by Wilderness through guest donations. The library now services all the villages in the Malama Chiefdom and provides the children with the opportunity to read, study and further their education.

Of Dust and Death

The buffalo is frequently referred to as one of Africa's most dangerous and formidable animals. Their bulk, strength and herd structure ensure that they are hunted by only the most opportunistic or specialised predators. Even the buffalo is vulnerable, though, and, as the dry season takes its toll with less and less nutritious forage and longer and longer distances to water, body condition and strength are sapped. It is then that lion take advantage, as on this occasion, in November at Kalamu Lagoon, when three lion (an adult female and her two young male offspring) pulled down two buffalo in one hunt.

144

Water, Worms and Trees
Back-of-house at Toka Leya Camp

In 2008, Wilderness won the concession to develop Toka Leya Camp in Mosi-oa-Tunya National Park. The location awarded through the tender had historically been the site of a village with associated fields, and was thus devoid of much natural vegetation. The large baobab tree on the north-western side of camp was the only indigenous tree that remained. In line with the Wilderness vision to restore conservation land, a plan was formulated to rehabilitate the once-flourishing flora.

Thus, in conjunction with ZAWA (Zambia Wildlife Authority), a Greenhouse and Nursery Project was started. Seeds and pods are collected from the National Park, germinated and their seedlings placed in the greenhouse to take root and grow. Once the seedlings have reached a certain height or age, they are re-potted and moved into the nursery.

The nursery is fertilised by compost and nitrate-rich "worm juice" produced by the camp's Worm Farm (which breaks down the kitchen's organic waste) and watered by waste water from the camp that has been filtered and treated by the Waste Water Treatment Plant.

The trees are then ready to be planted out around the camp, a process that sees leafy green return to the banks of the Zambezi and in which guests are encouraged to take part.

148

wildernessmalawi

Through Floodplain and Woodland

The herbivore herds of Liwonde

The Shire River is the lifeblood of Liwonde National Park. Originating in Lake Malombe, it flows languidly through the length of the Park, swelling and shrinking depending on the season. More than water, it brings with it fertile silt to the floodplains of this sanctuary; the open grasslands adjacent to the river host thousands of waterbuck, impala and warthog, while nearly 2 000 hippo harboured in the Shire River itself graze here at night. Herds of elephant and buffalo are drawn to both the grazing and water in this area, while species such as greater kudu, bushbuck and sable frequent the beautiful mopane woodlands away from the river. Sable occur here in densities rivalling the highest in Africa, travels through the woodland punctuated by the majestic jet-black coats of the males.

"My Supporting Factor"

Danford Manda in his own words

I come from Chintheche, a small village along the northern shores of Lake Malawi where Wilderness Safaris has a concession for Chintheche Inn on one of the Lake's most beautiful beaches. I am 22 years old and am the firstborn – of four – of one of the local families, with very little resources to live a proper life.

When I was 14, I used to see the children of Children in the Wilderness (CITW) meeting their mentors at Chihame Primary School near our home for follow-up meetings. I asked one of the mentors if I could join them and be registered as a member. Yes! I was accepted as a member of the CITW follow-up programme. This was in 2005. In 2006 I was recruited for that year's camp. I enjoyed every second of the camp week.

When I passed my primary-school exams I was selected to go to Chintheche Secondary School, but my parents could not afford to pay my school fees. They just could not do it. I aired my SOS to CITW for assistance and The Global Fund for Children sponsored my secondary education, which I completed by 2009.

My interest in Wilderness Safaris, which was initiated during my camp week, had grown by the time I finished school and I applied for any job with the company. My intention was to become a Safari Guide (they had inspired me a lot during my camp week), after which I had my sights set on becoming Camp Manager.

I started working for Wilderness Safaris in 2010 at Mvuu Camp as a trainee duty staff member. I worked very hard with great interest and it started to pay off this year (2011), when I was given a chance to become a trainee guide. I am learning things very quickly. I have no doubt that, by the end of this year, I will be a qualified full-time guide by Wilderness Safaris Malawi standards.

Since I started working with Wilderness Safaris, I have been the main financial supporter for my parents and young brothers and sisters. After understanding the importance of better education, I did not hesitate to start paying for the school needs of my two young sisters (Patricia and Loveness), who are now in secondary school. I am very proud that I am able to assist my two sisters in that way.

I thank CITW, Wilderness Safaris and The Global Fund for Children. They have been and they will be my supporting factor in all my successes in life.

Danford Manda – Mvuu Camp

Management through Research
Liwonde National Park aerial survey

Malawi's remaining wild areas are under huge pressure. A growing and already high-density rural population needs land for agriculture, firewood and other resources. In the competition between nature and people, people are winning the war; National Parks such as Liwonde are islands of wilderness in a rising sea of people. There is no doubt, though, that these islands are worth protecting. Aside from their biodiversity and value as ecosystems, they contribute to solutions through ecotourism and conservation employment as the most important local economic engine. To achieve this, however, it is critical that they are sustainably protected and managed, an important part of which is the annual aerial survey of large mammals.

For the past six years the Wilderness Wildlife Trust has helped fund a comprehensive aerial census of the large mammals of Liwonde. The results of these surveys have allowed stakeholders, such as Malawi's Department of National Parks and Wildlife, to gain an improved understanding of the Park's carrying capacity, trends in wildlife populations, threats to the Park's integrity and the effectiveness of management interventions.

Encouraging signs from the 2011 survey, conducted in October before the arrival of the rains, include continuing increases in elephant, buffalo, hippo, waterbuck, impala, warthog and sable. These findings, however, need to be balanced with an increasing trend in the illicit use of the Park area by neighbouring communities and a clear indication that more needs to be done to involve neighbouring people in the potential benefits of Liwonde.

160

Lake of Stars

"Lake of Stars" is the affectionate, somewhat whimsical, name given to Lake Malawi by missionary explorer Dr David Livingstone. While on its shores in the early 1860s, he watched nightly as the lanterns from fishermen's boats reflected on the black surface of the water, literally mirroring the effect of the stars from above. Today, nearly 16 million Malawians are still dependent on the Lake for protein. Fishing villages dot the shores, characterised by their distinctive drying racks, traditional dug-out canoes and other boats, and the ubiquitous sight of men mending fishing nets – all elements of lakeshore life.

wildernessmalawi

Returning the Forests
Chintheche Inn Reforestation Project

The ravages of deforestation cut through the hills and valleys of Malawi. Without electricity, charcoal – and the indigenous trees that it is made from – is the only source of energy for many. Chintheche Inn, through its Reforestation Project under the leadership of visionary nursery manager Master Banda, aims to replant the forests and more, to educate the people of the area.

Some years ago, a nursery was built on the Chintheche property to propagate seedlings for distribution, both for purposes of indigenous reforestation as well as for sustainable firewood use. These seedlings are provided free of charge to the area's environmental clubs. Each club is expected to mark the land, prepare the soil for planting and show that they have the necessary labour. Master Banda supervises the process personally and, once the seeds are planted, monitors each club closely to make sure that the young plants are well looked after. Education is also provided to the communities, teaching people how to use the trees in the most effective and sustainable way.

By the end of 2010, 15 clubs had been established and over 10 000 seedlings distributed. In 2011, the size of the nursery tripled. At this point, Children in the Wilderness Malawi became involved in the project, the children subsequently taking part in the process of tubing, seeding, distributing and planting. In 2011, Master Banda and the children managed to propagate over 25 000 trees of a variety of different species, which were distributed to over 50 community clubs and schools.

The project is at its busiest just before the rainy season (November to February), when the seedlings are prepared for distribution to the community tree sites. These sites are checked and the land pegged out; firebreaks are burned to protect existing sites with their sturdy year-old trees. When the rains begin, the seedlings are taken to their new homes. A forest is growing once more in Malawi.

Isolated Refuge
Nyika's bird diversity

The Nyika Plateau forms part of the Southern Rift Montane Forest-Grassland Mosaic and provides important, formally protected, refuge for a number of Southern Rift forest and grassland endemic birds. The grasslands provide habitat for species such as Churring and Black-lored Cisticola, Chapin's Apalis, Blue Swallow (Africa's largest breeding population at around 300 pairs), Jackson's Pipit, Scarlet-tufted Sunbird, Yellow-browed Seed-eater and Montane Widowbird. This unique ecosystem further hosts a number of endemic subspecies occurring nowhere else, which include Red-winged Francolin, Baglafecht Weaver and Rufous-naped Lark. Scrubby drainage lines within grassland are home to common residents such as Mountain Yellow Warbler, Ludwig's Double-collared Sunbird and Cinnamon Bracken Warbler.

Afromontane forest is confined to fire-sheltered valleys and watercourses. These forest patches, while relatively small, also offer equally impressive range-restricted bird diversity, such as the endemic Malawi Batis, Olive-flanked Robin-Chat, White-chested Alethe, the eye-catching Bar-tailed Trogon and Moustached Tinkerbird, skulking Fülleborne's Boubou, Mountain Thrush and chattering Southern Mountain Greenbul. Forest birding is often an exercise in patience and dogged determination, but the beauty of the forest interior and the birds when seen are their own reward.

This grassland-forest mosaic is unfortunately one of the most fragmented and threatened habitat types in Africa and lacks any significant formal protection – aside from the mountain fastness of the Nyika National Park.

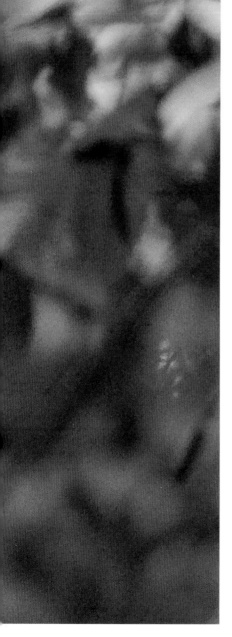

Predators of the Plateau

Wide open, high-altitude grasslands, evergreen forest patches and a distinctive prey population – ranging from diminutive red duiker and rock-loving klipspringer to roan and giant eland – dictate the unique complement of carnivores that hunt the Nyika Plateau. Long-legged, big-eared serval stalk the grasslands after dark, while side-striped jackal revel, wolf-like, in the open terrain, and arboreal large-spotted genet clamber through *Hagenia* thicket in search of prey. Leopards – spectacular in the heather-covered mountainous terrain – enjoy feline dominance in hunting reedbuck, bushbuck and the young of the larger species, but yield to clans of spotted hyaena that patrol the grasslands and hunt effectively in small packs.

wildernesssouthafrica

Marine Migrations
Whales and sharks of the Maputaland Marine Reserve

The warm waters just off Maputaland are home to a host of marine life, both large and small. Some of the most dramatic denizens, however, are seasonal visitors only: whales, dolphins, and sharks migrate along the coast – often close enough to shore to practically guarantee sightings of this great spectacle.

Winter (May to August) heralds the arrival of the leviathan humpback whales on their annual passage to their warm Indian Ocean calving grounds off Madagascar and Comoros; they head back south in autumn to arrive in the Antarctic – their summer feeding waters – by December. Southern right whales are also sometimes seen in winter and spring, their calving season taking place all around South Africa's coastline.

The onset of summer (October), and a subtle change of water temperature, signals the arrival of gamefish, whale sharks and ragged-tooth sharks. The fearsome-looking "raggies" are an annual highlight; the strangely docile, pregnant sharks migrate north into the area where they rest in caves hidden in the offshore coral reefs, often in waters only 10 metres deep. Their larger cousins, the whale sharks, are by contrast far more active, and move rapidly along the coast in their wide-ranging migrations. The numbers of this gentle giant and largest of fish (attaining lengths of up to 20 metres) are greatest off Mozambique and the KwaZulu-Natal coast of South Africa from October through April.

wildernesssouthafrica

Coastal Forest Creatures
Diminutive denizens of the vegetated dunes

The Maputaland Coastal Forest mosaic is characterised by a narrow strip of densely forested dunes that runs just inland, parallel to the Indian Ocean. These vegetated dunes, some of which rise imposingly up to 200 metres, are reputed to be the highest of their type in the world.

In contrast to the savannah, the area hosts a very different wildlife community when it comes to the resident birds, mammals, insects and flora. Here, it is the smaller things that count: the thrill of observing a secretive four-toed elephant shrew, for example, is equal to seeing a leopard in the savannah.

The diminutive red duiker and suni prefer the thicker forest, while the grey duiker ventures further into the coastal grasslands. Vervet monkeys and the rare samango are perfectly adapted to their arboreal existence in the forest canopies, while the alarm rants of a Tonga red squirrel often betray the presence of an African Goshawk perched nearby, or of a green mamba hidden in the foliage. Green Malkoha, Narina Trogon and Eastern Nicator are three special avian forest-dwellers.

The leaf litter is just as life-filled, with millipedes, foraging banded mongoose, the occasional water mongoose and even the subterranean yellow golden mole. It also provides the ideal habitat for the mesmerising but lethal Gaboon viper. Endangered blue duiker can be seen by the lucky few and Setaro's dwarf chameleon is found only in this dune system. After dark, nocturnal species, such as large spotted genet, thick-tailed bushbaby and African Wood-Owl, become more active – the vocalisations of the latter two being distinctive forest night sounds.

The butterflies are the real highlight of these dune forests, however. Cabbage whites flit daintily above the forest floor, while the dazzling gold-banded forester and green-banded swallowtail are just some of the nearly 200 butterfly species recorded in the iSimangaliso Wetland Park.

178

Painted Molluscs

Nudibranchs of the Indian Ocean

Divers of the Indian Ocean just off the Maputaland coast are often overwhelmed by the abundance and colour of life beneath the waves. And perhaps the most colourful and striking of all are the nudibranchs – a humble family of shell-less molluscs that have outclassed many larger species in an eye-catching array of creative shapes and hues.

The name "nudibranch" comes from the Latin *nudus* and Greek *branchia* and means "naked gills", as many display their gills on the outside of their bodies in the form of 'feathers' and other protuberances. These animals – also known as sea slugs – consist of some 3 000 species in warm shallow waters worldwide; carnivores, they hunt using tentacles and often derive their colouring from their prey. Their variation also shows in size – ranging from 60cm to less than 0.4cm – and longevity, where some live for just a month, while others have a year to brighten the ocean floor.

Coastal Cultures
The Mqobela and Mpukane Communities

One of the first joint ventures in South Africa between community, a conservation authority and an ecotourism enterprise was that of Rocktail Bay Lodge, built in the early 1990s. This innovative operating model involved Wilderness, the surrounding Mqobela and Mpukane communities and the iSimangaliso Wetland Park Authority. The success of such projects is dependent, however, upon continued long-term relationships between all parties; the Lodge's successor, Rocktail Beach Camp, opened in 2007 and enhanced the original model by creating a new structure that enables the community to participate more meaningfully.

Some 2% of the entire community are permanently employed at the camp, and guests are, as part of their activities, offered guided visits to the Mpukane community and the joint-venture Gugulesizwe Cultural Village in the rural coastal grasslands. Here, authentic aspects of Zulu culture and tradition can be observed through dance, architecture, food, traditional lifestyles and language.

These visits inform guests of the rich history of the coastal clans that fled to the area during the turbulent depredations of the *mfecane* (a chain of violent upheavals that occurred when the Zulu King Shaka subjugated vast territories in the early 19th century). Their ability to survive in the inhospitable environment of the coastal savannah, with its poor soils and pasturage, has helped them to maintain their socio-political and economic independence.

184

Healthy Predators, Healthy Prey
Pafuri's predator population growth

As apex predators, lion are a critical indicator of savannah ecosystem health. A healthy lion population implies a healthy prey population, which in turn suggests a healthy functioning ecosystem.

Of course, their place at the top of the food chain means that lion occur in far lower numbers than their prey, making the species vulnerable to local disturbances, such as disease, poaching or other factors. For whatever reason, this was the case at Pafuri in 2003 when Wilderness first entered into a partnership with the Makuleke Community. No lion were resident in the entire 24 000-hectare area and prey populations were significantly below historical levels.

Recognising the imbalance, Wilderness first set about removing any potential causes of artificial mortality (such as snares) and then, in partnership with the Kruger National Park, reintroduced supplementary populations of key prey species, such as impala, zebra and blue wildebeest. The result over the last eight years has been that the prey population has burgeoned and inevitably lion have recolonised the area and formed a stable pride structure: from no lion in 2003 to a healthy resident pride comprising four adult lionesses, two adult male lions and regular additions of cubs and subadults. Dispersing lion from other areas have also begun to enter the area and we anticipate the day when the roars of a second resident pride will echo through the Limpopo and Luvuvhu river valleys.

The growth in the lion population has been mirrored by an increase in numbers of other large carnivore species: leopard and spotted hyaena populations are growing, and there are even occasional sightings of species such as African wild dog.

Bushbaby Babies
Daytime sighting of a nocturnal newborn

The thick-tailed bushbaby, largest of the bushbaby family, is a primate but looks nothing like the monkeys and baboons that inhabit the Pafuri area; indeed it is a prosimian, a close relative of the earliest primates. A nocturnal species, it is more often heard than seen, with its eerie, plaintive cry (the reason for the name "bushbaby") echoing along the dense riverine forest of the Luvuvhu River where it makes its home.

One extremely hot October day at Pafuri, with the temperature hovering at 45 degrees Celsius, found guests seeking relief at the pool, under the shade of a Natal mahogany. It was while lounging and gazing lazily upwards that movement of a primate kind was seen through the leaves: large round eyes, long black skeletal fingers and almost transparent bat-shaped ears. A long bushy tail draped over the branch confirmed its identity as that of a thick-tailed bushbaby – and her three babies, all large milky eyes, enormous ears and tiny, delicate hands holding on firmly to her fur.

Bushbabies give birth to two to three young during the rainy months, in leaf nests built by the female. For the first few weeks of life, the young hold on to their mother, only letting go when she 'parks' them on a branch while she forages. This was an amazing sighting, firstly being a daytime one and, secondly, since during the day bushbabies rest up in trees, the young family wasn't going anywhere, allowing Pafuri guests to spend as long as they liked looking up through the leaves at the antics of these unusual and appealing creatures.

"All set about with Fever Trees"

Then Kolokolo Bird said, with a mournful cry, "Go to the banks of the great grey-green, greasy Limpopo River, all set about with fever trees, and find out."

Rudyard Kipling, The Elephant's Child

The forests of fever trees, along the low-lying floodplains of the Limpopo and Luvuvhu river systems at Pafuri, are unique in the Kruger National Park. Ghostly pale green trunks stretch up towards the light and form a closed canopy 15 to 20 metres above the ground. Below, the understorey is absent, leaving just a seasonal grass layer that allows good visibility. Thanks to this combination of light and colour, a strange aura permeates the forest.

Its unique atmosphere notwithstanding, sightings of species such as elephant, chacma baboons, zebra, nyala, greater kudu and buffalo are common, the trees providing nutrition for the browsers in the form of their flowers and leaves, and the seasonal grass layer sustaining the grazers.

Originally believed by early settlers to be a possible cause of malaria (because of its association with low-lying, sometimes swampy areas), this evocative species was immortalised as the fever tree by Rudyard Kipling in his *Just So Stories*, published in 1902. In xiTsonga, the language of the Makuleke on whose land Pafuri is located, the trees are known as *nkelenga* and, rather than associated with illness, are used in the treatment of burn wounds.

Neophytes in Nature
Children in the Wilderness – Pafuri Camp

Every year sees a number of Wilderness camps all over southern Africa being closed to paying guests for six days at a time in order to invite children from the neighbouring communities to take part in a Children in the Wilderness (CITW) camp. Pafuri Camp is no exception and, each December, hosts children from the Makuleke villages. In 2011, 40 children (21 girls and 19 boys) between the ages of 10 and 14 were selected from the four primary schools in the community to attend.

Although these children live in rural areas, most have never seen animals in their natural environment; for those that have, the encounter has usually been negative, such as an elephant raiding crops. What a change this is, as the children go on game drives in their historical homeland: eyes wide open and glued to binoculars, they gasp at every animal, big or small, and enthusiastically tick off birds in their notebooks and draw pictures of their favourite creature.

A particular highlight at Pafuri is the pride of the Makuleke people in their heritage and history. Their grandparents were forcibly removed from the area in 1969 until the late 1990s. On a visit to Deku – a large baobab where the chiefs and indunas of the community used to meet – they see tangible evidence of their past and learn of their people's return to become partners in conservation with Wilderness and the Kruger National Park.

For the first time in my life during camp I learn Lider Ship [leadership] Value
Mimie, 11 years old

A lasting memory of camp: The thing is the knowledge that I have got during camp and on game drives about taking care of animals, plants and environment.
Thabo, 13 years old

One thing I will always remember about camp: it is the Deku tree and fish eagle that was a beautiful bird at the Pafuri Camp
Nyiko, 12 years old

One thing I will always remember about camp: to wash a body in the barthroom
Myleen, 11 years old

wildernesskenya

Plateau of Plenty
Laikipia, Kenya

The grassy, acacia-dotted Laikipia Plateau, lying north of the iconic Aberdares and Mount Kenya mountains, is unique in Kenya. This 950 000-hectare (2.3 million-acre) mosaic of communities and private ranches is a melting pot of cultures and land uses, from low-density pastoralism (particularly cattle grazing) to both subsistence and commercial agriculture – as well as a growing number of conservation and wildlife areas. Amazingly, the area is home to Kenya's second highest concentration of wildlife after the Maasai Mara and certainly to its widest range of large mammal diversity, including a number of threatened species that have their stronghold here. It is also one of the few places where wildlife populations are actively increasing.

Whistling thorn scrub and woodland provides an abundance of nutrition to reticulated giraffe, elephant and eland. Impala use the ecotone between this and open grassland, and species such as plains and Grevy's zebra, Grant's and Thomson's gazelles, beisa oryx and Lelwel's hartebeest use the plains, often grazing in mixed herds below the silent gaze of the distant Mount Kenya. More secretive species such as waterbuck and bushbuck inhabit the river valleys and slightly thicker vegetation, but it is the sheer numbers of the herds that are so impressive.

The diversity of wildlife – a result of the range of habitats – mirrors the cultural diversity. Maasai, Turkana, Boran, Pokot, Samburu, Somali, Kikuyu and European people live side by side, all coexisting with the abundant big game that roams the Plateau.

The Sanctuary of Segera
Laikipia's wildlife corridor

In a world where wildlife areas are increasingly fragmented and isolated by fences or land use changes, the conservation of wildlife corridors that link habitats has become vital to the survival of many species: movement between their ranges allows seasonal access to the richest feeding areas – and therefore results in larger wildlife populations.

The position of Segera (and its size), as a link between the various parts of the Laikipia Plateau, forms one such critical conservation corridor between western and eastern Laikipia, enabling migratory movements by wide-ranging animals such as elephant, plains zebra, Grevy's zebra, wild dog and others – and the concomitant increase in their populations. The number of plains zebra on Segera at any one time, for example, exceeds a thousand animals, while the greater Laikipia elephant population also makes use of Segera to move between eastern and western and even northern and southern home ranges.

Such a pivotal location is Segera's primary contribution to biodiversity conservation, allowing it to connect isolated pockets of wildlife. In this way Segera is a sanctuary to a wide range, as well as large numbers, of wildlife, predators and prey alike.

wildernesskenya

The Honey Gatherers

Isolated on a remote portion of the Laikipia Plateau is a magnificent lone Shepherd's Tree – a honey gatherer's pride and joy.

Suspended on wires attached to the upper branches of the tree are 12 beehives. Resembling giant Bushman or San arrow quivers, they have hide covers on each end of a wooden tube to make a perfect hive. A few metres off the ground a large patch of tin, made from beaten corrugated iron, has been nailed to the trunk of the tree to stop honey badgers from raiding them.

The old man who owns the hives demonstrates how the honey would be extracted – he is now too old to climb trees, so his two sons help. They begin by splitting the wood from a *Euphorbia* into smaller shards, binding it together to make a parcel and lighting the contents. At this point one of the sons puts a blanket over his head and climbs the tree with a tin and the smoky, smouldering parcel. Reaching the first hive, he removes the hide cover and blows smoke into it. The smoke appears to anaesthetise the bees and they all start moving to the other side of the hive.

After a few minutes the hive is largely vacated and the climber gathers the honeycombs and drops them into the tin, being careful to leave sufficient comb inside the hive for the bees. At no time does he seem to be stung. When he has enough honey, he closes up the hive and climbs down the tree. Beautiful to taste, the light brown honey is sold in the community, both to be eaten and as the basis for a potent liquor.

The tree has been in the family for years, handed down from father to son, and is an example of the sustainable use of a natural resource through traditional means.

"Acting today for a better tomorrow"
The Zeitz Foundation

The vision of Segera is to create a self-sustaining, responsible conservation model, which preserves a part of Kenya's natural heritage, benefits the local population, enhances ecotourism and promotes sustainable land use, while creating jobs, encouraging education, art and awareness of conservation issues.

Much of this noble and visionary work is performed by the Zeitz Foundation which has its international headquarters at Segera. Aside from wildlife management and monitoring, including of priority species such as the Grevy's zebra (Endangered), the Foundation also engages with neighbouring rural communities in a broad range of social and conservation activities. These range from promoting income-generating opportunities based on the sustainable use of natural resources and traditional skills, to environmental education activities, including the use of theatre, to raise awareness of conservation issues.

Support is also provided in the form of local infrastructure such as schools and clinics, while a key objective is to promote peace and unity in Laikipia via such projects as the Laikipia Unity Cup, a biennial football tournament. By utilising the unifying power of this sport, more than 20 000 people throughout Laikipia are brought together, working to improve environmental management, deliver health care and build peace and unity throughout the district.

wildernessseychelles

A Fragile Filigree
Coral reefs of North Island

The myriad shapes and colours of coral reefs are synonymous with warm tropical oceans and swarming marine biodiversity. Indeed, coral reefs harbour some 25% of all marine life and are critical spawning grounds for many species of fish.

This filigree fantasy world is a fragile one, however. Corals are actually the result of a symbiotic relationship between polyps and algae, the polyps benefiting nutritionally from the photosynthetic algae. But their need for sunlight proved to be the undoing of corals in Seychelles during the coral bleaching of the late 1990s. Warmer surface sea temperatures – a result of global warming – caused the polyps to reject the algae and ultimately to die; their bleached white skeletons are all that remain of previously vibrant reefs.

Over the intervening decade North Island has participated in regular reef monitoring to track the recovery of the reefs, a process that has resulted in the reappearance of both hard and soft corals such as daisy, lettuce and staghorn coral, as well as palmate sea fans. Slowly, the undersea gardens are returning to their former abundance.

wilderness seychelles

Barefoot Luxury

Since its opening in 2003, North Island has become renowned as one of the world's most spectacular tropical islands, its luxurious accommodation, menu and service winning many awards. Each of the 11 individually handcrafted guest villas has been constructed to create a sensorial experience in surroundings of understated elegance, with the unique atmosphere and distinct flavour of the Seychelles.

Its signature style is known as "barefoot luxury", a concept that combines natural beauty with sheer luxury.

In a world where, all too often, indulgence is reached at the expense of the environment, Wilderness' commitment to the renewal of the natural processes of North Island, while at the same time creating the ultimate in island hospitality – in effect placing luxury in harmony with Nature – is a rare experience indeed.

222

Renewed Haven
Resurrection of a tropical island refuge

Oceanic islands are often refuges and nesting grounds for seabirds and other species, especially if they are located near productive feeding grounds. The lack of predators means that birds tend to nest on the ground, free from egg or chick predation. This delicate balance can be rudely interrupted and upset when new predators, such as ship rats, domestic cats and snakes, invade and colonise islands.

This has been the case in Seychelles, where populations of ground-nesting birds, such as the Wedge-tailed Shearwater, White-tailed Tropicbird and Fairy Tern, have suffered as a result. Even populations of endemic reptile species, such as the Seychelles skink and stripeless day gecko, have declined.

The removal of unnatural predators from North Island has resulted in a pleasing resurrection of indigenous life. Several tropicbird pairs now breed on the island, shearwaters nest colonially on a granite outcrop, and a resident Seychelles Kestrel pair uses another. Today, Seychelles Blue Pigeons are a common sight, and even the skinks and geckos have recovered their numbers.

A Vegetable Garden of Eden

In the middle of North Island, the tangle of palms, takamaka trees and lush riotous undergrowth gives way to the hub of the island's workings: the staff village, the nursery – where thousands of indigenous seeds are being nurtured until they are large enough to be replanted across the island – and the organic vegetable garden.

Rows of tall eggplants, tomato bushes, maize and beetroot, to name but a few, are tangible proof not only of the island's incredible return to fertility (after years as a coconut plantation that leached the nutrients of the soil), but also of the goal that, one day, most vegetables and fruit on the menu will no longer be brought by barge from Mahé, but will be grown right here, organically and locally.

"Chasing my dream"

Elliot Mokhobo

Elliot started working on North Island in 2002 as part of the construction crew, later moving into maintenance. In 2009, he joined the Environment Department and currently has a variety of roles including guiding guests, maintaining hiking trails, pest control and the capture of various research data. He is best known for his commitment to turtle conservation: he monitors the females when they emerge to lay eggs on the beach, and he patrols the beach daily to check on the resulting nests.

It was on the 19th of May 2002 that I arrived on North Island from South Africa as a labourer to help build the villas on the Island, to make a beautiful place for guests to come to. As breadwinner and father of four children I was thrilled to be able to have work – and overseas as well! Since then, I have become a professional guide with the environmental team on North Island. I love to explain to the guests about the turtles, how they lay eggs, and the hatching process. If turtles are hatching, I try to call any guests that are on the Island to come and see this amazing sight.

I believe I am fulfilling a purpose by working here on North Island – so that people can come and enjoy this island and learn to love nature at the same time.

But for me the most important thing is that I keep on learning. Even at age 56, it's never too late to learn. That's why I am now busy becoming a divemaster! When I came to the Island I knew how to swim but not how to dive. So I asked if I could snorkel and I did this for a year before I saw that it's no use just to snorkel; one is standing still in the same place! So I asked permission to learn to dive and the manager at the time said I could. I was the first staff member (aside from the divers) who learnt how to dive.

In life, when I wake up in the morning, I can go back to sleep or I can chase after my dream. And my dream is to study more, learn more and to work with people from all over the world to do the best I can for me, my family and for the North Island and all the people and animals on it.

Elliot Mokhobo – North Island

Acknowledgements

We would like to thank everyone involved in the creation of this book, the second in our series on our African wilderness areas and their diversity. **Copy:** Martin Benadie, Chris Roche and Ilana Stein. **Editing and proofreading:** Eleanor Mary Cadell, Caroline Culbert, Monica Jooste, Warren Ozorio and Mary-Anne van der Byl. **Design and layout:** Ulrike van der Hoven. **Image selection and pre-press colour:** Mike Myers. Our gratitude also goes to the photographers (credited below), our dedicated field and office staff, our long-term partners in the travel industry and, most importantly, our guests with whom we have shared these beautiful ecosystems.

Captions and Photographers

All images captioned clockwise across pages from top left.

COVER — Carmine Bee-eater flock at nesting colony near Kings Pool King, Linyanti, Botswana (Grant Atkinson).

WILDERNESS PHILOSOPHY

Pages 1-2: African Skimmer flock over the Kafue River, Zambia (Dana Allen).

Pages 3-4: Foraging African Skimmer, Kafue, Zambia (Dana Allen).

WILDERNESS MOMENTS

Pages 5-6: Mokoro expedition, Jacana Camp, Okavango, Botswana (Dana Allen).

Pages 7-8: Aerial view of Busanga Bush Camp and red lechwe herd, Kafue, Zambia (Mike Myers).

Pages 9-10: Tropical island escape, North Island, Seychelles (Michael Poliza).

Pages 11-12: Guided walk on the floodplains, Jao Camp, Okavango, Botswana (Dana Allen).

Pages 13-14: Guide and young guests, Shumba Camp, Kafue, Zambia (Cardo Kleberg).

Pages 15-16: Lion pride on zebra kill, Tubu Tree Camp, Okavango, Botswana (Dana Allen).

Pages 17-18: Lanner Gorge sunrise, Pafuri Camp, Kruger, South Africa (Dana Allen).

Pages 19-20: Wilderness Air Cessna Caravan over Sossusvlei, Namibia (Dana Allen).

Pages 21-22: Picnic brunch, Jao Camp, Okavango, Botswana (Dana Allen).

Pages 23-24: Kalamu Star-bed Camp, South Luangwa, Zambia (Dana Allen).

Pages 25-26: Bird watching guide and guest, Xigera Camp, Okavango, Botswana (Dana Allen).

Pages 27-28: Early morning hot air balloon, Shumba Camp, Kafue, Zambia (Mike Myers).

Pages 29-30: Himba cultural interaction, Serra Cafema Camp, Marienfluss, Namibia (Dana Allen).

Pages 31-32: After-dinner stargazing, Little Kulala, Sossusvlei, Namibia (Dana Allen).

Pages 33-34: Coffee around the fire at dawn, Shumba Camp, Kafue, Zambia (Michael Poliza).

Pages 35-36: Shire River boat ride, Mvuu Camp, Liwonde, Malawi (Dana Allen).

WILDERNESS CONGO

Pages 37-38: Misty morning at Lango Bai, Odzala (Mike Myers).

Pages 39-40: Forest giant (Chris Roche); guereza colobus (Tim Jackson – *Africa Geographic*); forest walk (Mike Myers).

Pages 41-42: Early morning mist rising from the Lekoli River, Odzala (Mike Myers).

Pages 43-44: Forest elephant bull (Tim Jackson – *Africa Geographic*); forest buffalo herd (Mike Myers).

Pages 45-46: African Grey Parrots (Tim Jackson – *Africa Geographic*); African Green-Pigeons (Mike Myers); African Green-Pigeon feeding frenzy (Tim Jackson – *Africa Geographic*).

Pages 47-48: Circling African Green-Pigeon flock, Lango Bai, Odzala (Mike Myers).

Pages 49-50: Gorilla tracking; Dr Magda Bermejo explaining gorilla behaviour; silverback gorilla; subadult female gorilla (Mike Myers x4); curious young male gorilla (Tim Jackson – *Africa Geographic*).

Pages 51-52: Subadult female western lowland gorilla of the Neptuno Group, Ndzehi, Odzala (Mike Myers).

Pages 53-54: Female glider *Cymothoe sp*; forester *Euphaedra sp.*; pale babul blue *Azanus mirza*; Cameroun branded blue *Uranothauma flakensteini* (Sandra Schonbachler x4).

Pages 55-56: Butterfly flock (forest leopard *Phalanta eurytus*, spotted lilac tree nymph *Sevenia pechueli* and yellow *Urema sp.*) in forest clearing, Likeni, Odzala (Mike Myers).

WILDERNESS NAMIBIA

Pages 57-58: Desert-adapted black rhino bull, cow and calf, Desert Rhino Camp, Palmwag (Olwen Evans).

Pages 59-60: Namibia's diverse Herero, Nama and Damara communities, Damaraland (Olwen Evans x6).

Pages 61-62: Himba women and settlement, Serra Cafema Camp, Marienfluss (Mike Myers).

Pages 63-64: Turner's gecko, Sossusvlei (Dana Allen); common barking gecko, Sossusvlei (Dana Allen); Namib rock agama, Damaraland (Dana Allen); ground agama, Damaraland (Caroline Culbert); Boulton's Namib day gecko (Dana Allen).

Pages 65-66: Black-backed jackal kill springbok only to lose it to a male lion coalition, Etosha (Richard van der Wel x4).

Pages 67-68: Typical dry-season waterhole scene, Etosha (Simon Hartinger).

Pages 69-70: White-tailed Shrike nest and chicks, Andersson's Camp, Ongava (Martin Benadie x4).

Pages 71-72: Dr Sam Nujoma, former president of Namibia, opens the camp (Jennifer Lalley); dignitaries greet Doro Nawas staff (Jennifer Lalley); excited staff members (Olwen Evans); commemorative plaque (Jennifer Lalley).

Pages 73-74: Desert-adapted elephant herd crossing barren plain, Damaraland Camp, Damaraland (Olwen Evans).

Pages 75-76: Rare scene of a water-filled Sossusvlei; Damaraland swathed in green; Etosha in summer (Dana Allen x3).

Pages 77-78: Rain and clouds advance across the dunes, Kulala Desert Lodge, Sossusvlei (Dana Allen).

WILDERNESS BOTSWANA

Pages 79-80: Male leopard crossing the Savute Channel, Savuti Camp, Linyanti (Mike Myers).

Pages 81-82: Jumping spider; African Jacana; African Pygmy-Goose; Angolan reed frog (Dana Allen x4); flap-necked chameleon (Grant Atkinson); adult male sitatunga (Derek de la Harpe).

Pages 83-84: Aerial view of the Okavango Delta near Little Vumbura Camp (Mike Myers).

Pages 85-86: Female wild dog regurgitating for black-backed jackals (Mike Myers); wild dog with spotted hyaena and black-backed jackal (Russel Friedman); wild dog and jackals on the hunt; wild dog 'mothering' black-backed jackal pups (Ryan Green x2).

Pages 87-88: Photovoltaic solar panel array, Xigera Camp, Okavango Delta (Dana Allen).

Pages 89-90: Banded mongoose mother and baby (Grant Atkinson); yellow mongoose; slender mongoose (Mike Myers x2).

Pages 91-92: Saddle-billed Stork (Dana Allen); Squacco Heron (Martin Benadie); Malachite Kingfisher (Dana Allen); Rufous-bellied Heron (Dana Allen).

Pages 93-94: African Spoonbills forage amongst day waterlilies, Chitabe Camp, Okavango Delta (Caroline Culbert).

Pages 95-96: Warona the elephant calf, Abu Camp, Okavango (Brennan Rimer x6 – *Journeys Unforgettable*).

Pages 97-98: Botswana guide training: approaching game on foot; identifying tracks; tree identification; theoretical lecture; boat maintenance (Dana Allen x5).

Pages 99-100: Brown hyaena (Mike Myers); foraging honey badger (Grant Atkinson); Cape fox pups (Clive Dreyer); bat-eared fox (Clive Dreyer).

Pages 101-102: Male cheetah coalition, Deception Valley, Central Kalahari (Grant Atkinson).

WILDERNESS ZIMBABWE

Pages 103-104: Lions decide discretion is the better part of valour, Davison's Camp, Hwange (Mike Myers).

Pages 105-106: Yellow-billed Stork and Marabou Stork competition, Ruckomechi Camp, Mana Pools (Kevin van Breda x4).

Pages 107-108: Curious African wild dog pups; affectionate lionesses; male leopard (Kevin van Breda x3).

Pages 109-110: Burchell's zebra herd on dry-season Ngamo Plains, Hwange (Mike Myers).

Pages 111-112: Lone blue wildebeest bull silhouetted on Ngamo Plains, Hwange (Dana Allen).

Pages 113-114: Wistful cheetah cub; subadult cheetah wait patiently in woodland for their mother; male cheetah marking territory (Dana Allen x3).

Pages 115-116: Subadult cheetah using termite mound as vantage point in woodland, Little Makalolo Camp, Hwange (Dana Allen).

Pages 117-118: Ziga School and vegetable garden in Ziga Village, Hwange (Liz Lane x2).

Pages 119-120: Elephant bull; elephant calf; elephant bull at mineral lick; elephant herd drinking (Dana Allen x4).

Pages 121-122: Elephant breeding herd emerges from the woodland en route to a waterhole, Little Makalolo Camp, Hwange (Dana Allen).

WILDERNESS ZAMBIA

Pages 123-124: Wattled Crane pair with sable antelope herd in background, Busanga Bush Camp, Kafue (Dana Allen).

Pages 125-126: Lightning and advancing summer thunderstorm, Shumba Camp, Kafue (Dana Allen).

Pages 127-128: Dominant male lion crossing the Busanga Plains ahead of looming storm clouds, Shumba Camp, Kafue (Dana Allen).

Pages 129-130: Southern reedbuck; puku; roan antelope; sitatunga; red lechwe (Dana Allen x5).

Pages 131-132: Aerial view of red lechwe herds dotted across the northern Busanga Plains, Busanga Bush Camp, Kafue (Mike Myers).

Pages 133-134: Vet administering sedative; taking of blood sample; measurement of canines; lion research team; fitting satellite collar (Dana Allen x5).

Pages 135-136: Böhm's Flycatcher; Pale-billed Hornbill; Rufous-bellied Tit; Souza's Shrike; Green-capped Eremomela; Arnot's Chat; Red-capped Crombec (Martin Benadie x7).

Pages 137-138: Lichtenstein's hartebeest herd in leafless miombo woodland, Kafue (Martin Benadie).

Pages 139-140: Clash between two hippopotamus bulls in the Luangwa River, Kalamu Lagoon Camp, South Luangwa (Dana Allen).

Pages 141-142: Kalengo Village School; village children; community survey with female household head; village life in the Malama Chiefdom (Sue Snyman x4).

Pages 143-144: Lioness tests buffalo herd; lioness and young male isolate buffalo cow; another pride member catches and kills a buffalo calf; lioness surveying the aftermath (Dana Allen x4).

Pages 145-146: Buffalo cow eventually overwhelmed by lion, Kalamu Lagoon Camp, South Luangwa (Dana Allen).

Pages 147-148: Seed germination in the greenhouse; sapling planted in camp grounds; sapling being planted; selection of sapling; explanation of worm farm (Caroline Culbert x5).

Pages 149-150: White-fronted Bee-eater colony, Toka Leya Camp, Zambezi River (Caroline Culbert).

wilderness acknowledgements

WILDERNESS MALAWI

Pages 151-152: Zebra herd silhouetted against cumulonimbus cloud over the Nyika Plateau, Chelinda Lodge, Nyika (Dana Allen).

Pages 153-154: Hippo cow and calf (Martin Benadie); impala herd and waterbuck on Shire River floodplain (Dana Allen); inquisitive sable (Dana Allen).

Pages 155-156: Elephant herd drinking along Shire River, Mvuu Lodge, Liwonde (Dana Allen).

Pages 157-158: Danford Manda (Etienne Rochat); typical game drive experience, Mvuu Lodge (Dana Allen).

Pages 159-160: Single elephant bull near Shire River (Dana Allen); buffalo herd in woodland (Frank Weitzer).

Pages 161-162: Lakeside life: fish drying racks; homemade guitar; traditional fishing dugout; child carrying maize; boys preparing boat; washing up duties (Dana Allen x5).

Pages 163-164: CITW children choose seedlings (Symon Chibaka); the Chintheche Nursery (Caroline Culbert); CITW child cares for seedling (Symon Chibaka); Master Banda at home with his precious plants (Caroline Culbert).

Pages 165-166: Rufous-naped Lark (Dana Allen), Yellow-browed Seed-eater (Martin Benadie); Chapin's Apalis (Dana Allen); Malawi Batis (Martin Benadie); Bar-tailed Trogon (Dana Allen).

Pages 167-168: Endemic subspecies of Red-winged Francolin, Chelinda Lodge, Nyika (Mike Myers).

Pages 169-170: Male leopard; side-striped jackal; serval (Dana Allen x3).

Pages 171-172: Spotted hyaena, nose flared, peers from bracken, Chelinda Lodge, Nyika (Mike Myers).

WILDERNESS SOUTH AFRICA

Pages 173-174: Zebra, impala and buffalo dot the fertile floodplain of the Limpopo River, Pafuri Camp, Kruger (Dana Allen).

Pages 175-176: Humpback whale breaching (Dana Allen x3); female ragged-tooth shark (Karen Deller); whale shark with remoras attached to underside (Anthony Grote).

Pages 177-178: Water mongoose (Geoff Nichols); African Goshawk (Martin Benadie); gold-banded forester (Martin Benadie); thick-tailed bushbaby (Dana Allen); red duiker (Dana Allen); large spotted genet (Dana Allen).

Pages 179-180: Green-banded swallowtail, Rocktail Beach Camp, Maputaland (Martin Benadie).

Pages 181-182: Colourful nudibranchs, Rocktail Beach Camp, Maputaland (Jess Wall x3; Antony Grote x1).

Pages 183-184: Nguni cattle on the shores of Lake Sibaya (Russel Friedman); young girl pumping water (Mike Myers); traditional sangoma (Dana Allen).

Pages 185-186: Traditional Zulu dancing at Gugulesizwe Cultural Village, Rocktail Beach Camp, Maputaland (Dana Allen).

Pages 187-188: Spotted hyaena (Dana Allen); African wild dog (Caroline Culbert); leopard (Dana Allen).

Pages 189-190: Dominant male lion of the Pafuri Pride in daytime repose, Pafuri Camp, Kruger (Callum Sargent).

Pages 191-192: Adult female thick-tailed bushbaby holds her three offspring; one mischievous youngster wriggles free to peer down (Caroline Culbert x2).

Pages 193-194: Elephant bull with distinctive green fever tree smudge on trunk (Mike Myers); buffalo herd grazing in fever tree forest (Tina Sears).

Pages 195-196: Excited CITW children on game drive; lessons in the field; playtime in the swimming pool; the thrill of a game drive (Brett Wallington x4).

Pages 197-198: Children in the Wilderness: A new way of seeing the natural world, Pafuri Camp, Kruger (Brett Wallington).

WILDERNESS KENYA

Pages 199-200: Two elephant bulls crossing the savannah below Mount Kenya, Segera Retreat, Laikipia (Kate Potgieter-Vos).

Pages 201-202: Grant's gazelle (Derek de la Harpe); reticulated giraffe (Mike Myers).

Pages 203-204: Plains (Burchell's) zebra crossing open grassland on the Laikipia Plateau, Segera Retreat, Laikipia (Mike Myers).

Pages 205-206: Elephant herd drinking (Jochen Zeitz); beisa oryx herd (Mike Myers); Grevy's zebra (Kate Potgieter-Vos).

Pages 207-208: Quizzical male leopard, Segera Retreat, Laikipia (Mike Myers).

Pages 209-210: Honey collectors gather below their hives; men proudly displaying the fruits of their labour; sealed end of a hive; setting the *Euphorbia* bundle alight; binding *Euphorbia* cuttings together (Mike Myers x5).

Pages 211-212: Honey gatherer smoking out bees from a traditional artificial hive, Segera Retreat, Laikipia (Mike Myers).

Pages 213-214: School headmaster in office decorated with pledges of unity and tolerance; dedicated students and teacher in rural classroom (Mike Myers x2).

Pages 215-216: Environmentally-themed theatre embraces oral tradition, educates, entertains and unites communities, Segera Retreat, Laikipia (Mike Myers).

WILDERNESS SEYCHELLES

Pages 217-218: Idyllic palm-fringed beach scene from Villa 9, North Island (Dana Allen).

Pages 219-220: Colourful array of hard and soft corals on reefs off North Island (Patrick Armstrong x5).

Pages 221-222: Cascading levels of Villa North Island meet the beach, North Island (Mike Myers).

Pages 223-224: Romantic isolation on Honeymoon Beach, North Island (Dana Allen).

Pages 225-226: Seychelles Blue Pigeon (Mike Myers); Seychelles White-eye (Mike Myers); stripeless day gecko (Dana Allen); White-tailed Tropicbird (Mike Myers).

Pages 227-228: Stripeless day gecko, *Phelsuma sp.*, in re-established indigenous vegetation, North Island (Mike Myers).

Pages 229-230: Chef gathering fresh ingredients in the island vegetable garden; from the garden straight to the table (Andrew Howard x2).

Pages 231-232: Elliot Mokhobo and environmental manager, Linda Vanherck, investigate a hatched turtle nest (Ilana Stein); Elliot Mokhobo (Mike Myers).

Pages 233-234: Aerial view of North Island from the north. Silhouette and Mahé Islands are visible in the background (Mike Myers).